Complete Guide of Lyon

Paul den Arend

Book design and production by Free Tour Lyon
Editing by Paul den Arend

Published by: Free Tour Lyon, 69007 Lyon

CONTENTS

1. Introduction

Lyon is one of my favorite cities in France. It is often overlooked by tourists, but completely without reason. The city has a long and interesting history and the historic center is beautiful. There is such a nice contrast between the current city center, Presqu'île and the old heart of the city, Vieux Lyon. Presqu'île looks very French, almost Parisian. Here you see the beautiful white 19th century façades that are typical of French architecture. Then, when you cross the Saône river, you find yourself in the second biggest renaissance area after Venice. In Vieux Lyon, the colors of the city change. Gone is the white of Presqu'île. Here you see Italian colors; red, yellow and gold. You can clearly see the influence of Italy and its traders and bankers on this old part of the city.

Lyon has always been a trading city. It was probably the most important city in France for the Romans. All the roads that they constructed in France started here. Lyon is built on a very strategic spot. It lies close to Italy, but not in the Alps. Two rivers join here and a hill provides shelter from attackers. This has made this city perfect for trading with Italy. This trade has brought Lyon prosperity, a prosperity that continues to this day. The economic area around Lyon is the second biggest in France, after the Île-de-France area around Paris. It is a hub for science, commerce and art.

If you bought this book, I assume you are planning a trip to Lyon. You will not be disappointed. The city has many highlights. There is the beautiful area of Vieux Lyon, the sumptuous Presqu'île and the very modern Confluence. There are lush parks, long riverbanks and superb museums. And then there is the food. Lyon is the culinary capital of France and food is something the Lyonnais adore. They love eating out and they love cooking themselves. Make sure to try some traditional dishes when you visit.

My name is Paul. I am a tour guide and currently living in Lyon. I guide groups around here. I operate a small tour company called Free Tour Lyon. I provide daily guided tours throughout Lyon. If you want to join one of my tours, you can go to my website www.freetourlyon.com.

I hope you enjoy this quick guide of the most important highlights in Lyon.

If you want to contact me for any reason, please feel free. You can send me an email on p.den.arend@zoho.com.

2. Vieux Lyon

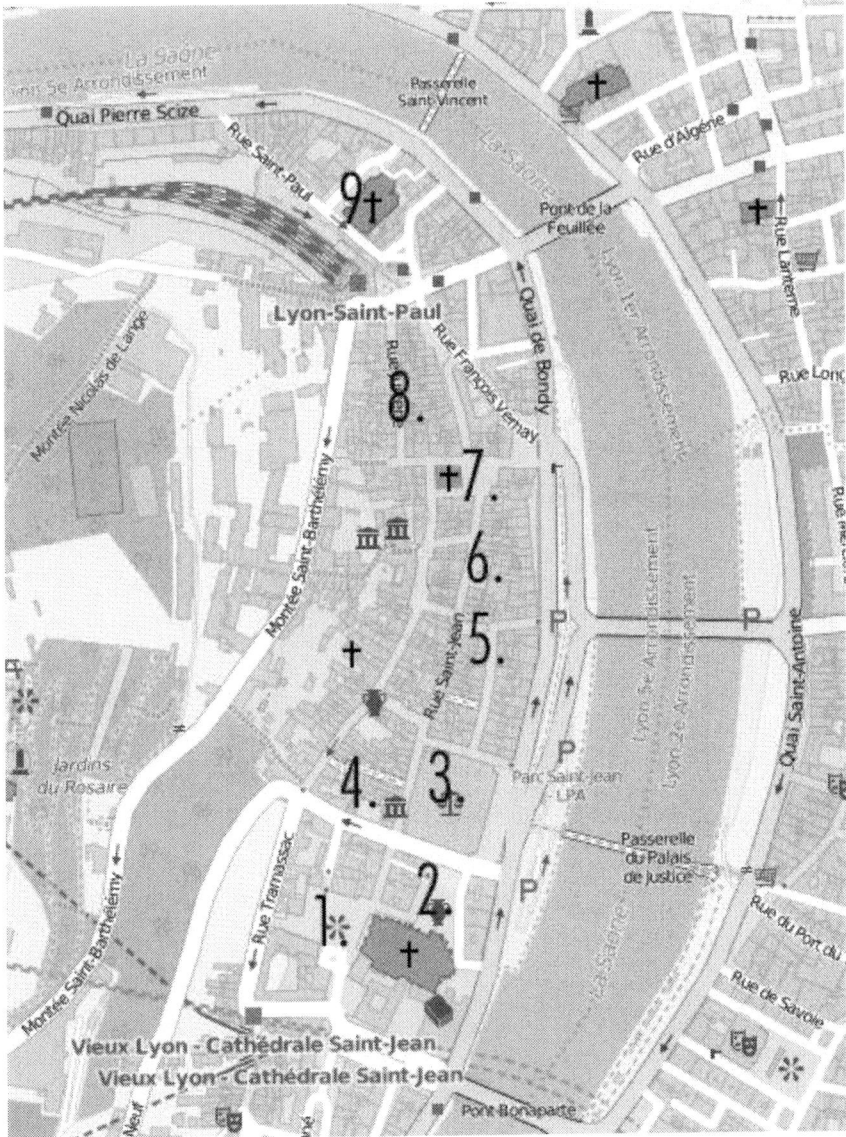

1. Place Saint-Jean
2. Archeolgical garden
3. Palais de Justice
4. Maison des Avocats
5. Place de la Baleine
6. Place du Gouvernement
7. Place du Change
8. Rue Juiverie
9. Saint Paul

Place Saint Jean

In Vieux Lyon, there is more than a thousand years of history between the houses. Vieux Lyon used to be the city during the middle ages and the renaissance. It became rich thanks to the trade fairs that often took place during those times. Lyon was the main hub for trade with Italy and in those times and Italy was the trading hub of the world. Spices and exotic goods were imported through Venice and Florence was a main producer of fine cloth. If French or English kings and nobility wanted to buy these goods, it first had to pass through Lyon.

Now Vieux Lyon is a UNESCO world Heritage site. It is the biggest renaissance area in France and the second in Europe, after Venice.

Saint Jean Cathedral

This cathedral is dedicated to John the Baptist. 300 years were needed to construct it. It was started in Romanesque style and finished in the Gothic style. It is the most important church in Lyon. The archbishop of Lyon has the title of Primat des Gaules, which means 'The first of the Gauls'. This is because Lyon was the first diocese of France.

On the facade you can see 300 medallions with scenes from the bible and of daily life. Go a bit close to check them out. Nobody ever seems to look at them, but some are very nice. See if you can recognize some scenes from the bible. It should not be too hard!

Around the main door, you can see mostly scenes from the bible, like the stories of Adam and Eve, Noah, Moses etc. Around the side doors, you will see many funny, strange and sometimes scary scenes. You will see many monsters, knights and scenes from antiquity. It might seem strange to find these stories here, because they are not very Christian. You often find these kinds of scenes on the outside of gothic churches. These were the stories, legends and fairytales that people would tell each other. They have a place on the church, but always on the outside and often next to the side doors.

Also notice how a lot of the angels in the arch around the main door miss their heads. These were destroyed by a German mercenary army during the religious wars of the 15th century.

During the Middle Ages Lyon was the most visited city in France by the popes, after Avignon (which belonged to the Papal States). Clement V was even crowned in this church. On this occasion, a wall on the nearby hill fell down. Onlookers fled, the Pope fell and lost one of the precious stones on his tiara. The stone was never recovered.

Inside, you can see that the cathedral is not very richly decorated. The choir and apse were recently completely restored. The most interesting artifact inside the cathedral is the astronomical clock from the fourteenth century.

It is nine meters tall and indicates the position of the moon, sun, stars and earth (besides of course the time). The last restauration in 1954 reset the clock's calendar and it will now be accurate until 2019. Then, it will have to be reset again. At the moment the clock is not working. This is because of the big restauration of the Cathedral. If you look at the front part of the inside of the Church, you will notice this part still needs restauration. The back part of the Church, around the apse and altar, is already restored. Notice how it looks much cleaner.

During the restauration, the clock stopped. Dust went inside the mechanism. Now, we are waiting for the restauration to finish to restart the clock and clean it.

There are some beautiful side chapels on the south side of the

Cathedral. Notice the beautiful stained glass windows. There are quite a few windows that are original from the 13th century, but also new ones. It's easy to see which ones are new, they look more like abstract artworks. When the Germans retreated during the second world war, they blew up the bridges over the Saône river. This damaged a lot of stained glass windows in the church.

Try to go inside the Bourbon chapel. This one should be open. The gothic architecture is quite beautiful, but the stained glass window looks like a blue, abstract artwork. Also notice the impressive baroque painting of the Three Kings.

Archeological garden

Around the corner from the church, there is a small archeological garden. Here you can see the remains of some of the oldest churches in Lyon. The church in Lyon is the oldest in the West, after Rome. The first church was established here in 150 A.D.

Here you can see two churches: Saint Croix and Saint-Etienne. These remains were discovered in the 1970, when the houses that stood here were demolished.

The foundations of Saint-Etienne, the church closest to the cathedral, are very interesting. These foundations go back to the 4th century. This means this church was built just a few decades after the legalization of Christianity by emperor Constantine in 313.

You can still see the remains of the old baptistry font underneath the glass. Notice that it's very big. This was very common in the 4th century. People were often adults when they converted and had to go in all the way to be baptized. Also, the baptistery was located outside of the main church. The reason is that you were not allowed inside the main church unless you were baptized. You see the same in Italy. The baptistry in Florence is in front of the Duomo, the baptistery in Pisa is outside the Cathedral and in Rome, you can find the baptistery of Saint John Lateran outside the church.

Maison du Chamarier

The Chamarier was the magistrate in charge of finances in the 1500s. He collected the taxes from the many trade fairs and got rich in the process. Now there is a famous Bakery here, on Rue Saint-Jean. Notice the bags of *pralines*, the bags of bright pink nuts. These are very typical of the city. The best way to try them is to get a *brioche à pralines*, a brioche bun filled with pralines.

If the door to the courtyard is open, please feel free to have a look around. Often, the courtyards are the most impressive part of the houses. This one is quite spectacular, with a lovely, almost classical well, designed by Philibert Delorme.

When you walk in, have a look back up. You can see a beautifully frescoed ceiling in one of the passageways on top. Also, notice the richly decorated well. A well was the symbol of wealth in the middle ages. If you had your own well in your own courtyard, you did not have to go to the river for your drinking water, like the poor people would have to do. Many of the courtyards you will visit on a tour of Vieux Lyon have wells and they are always a symbol of wealth.

Maison Des Avocats

This is one of the most photographed spots in all of Lyon. You can clearly see the influence of Italy and the Italian renaissance on the city. The colors of the houses seem to come straight out of Tuscany. In the 14th century there was a stage coach inn here. You can still see the big opening to the courtyard, where the coaches could come in. The outer wall has disappeared though.

You can see twelve Tuscan arches from 1516. After, this became a school for lawyers. Now it is the museum of cinema and miniatures, which is more fun than it sounds.

The Miniature museum was founded by Dan Ohlman. He was an interior designer from Paris, who, in his free time, designed *miniatures*. Newspapers started writing about him and he started doing little exhibitions around France. When he came to Lyon, his exhibition on Place Saint-Jean was a great success and he decided to stay in Lyon. He started a little museum in Rue Juiverie and a few years after managed to open up here.

The museum is really fun. He collects miniatures and restores artifacts from Hollywood movies. Often, in the morning, I see a new crate coming through the gate. He has the mask from The Mask, batman costumes from batman movies and whole sets from the movie The Perfume. You can easily spend hours here.

La Longue Traboule

Lyon is famous for its many traboules. Traboules are walkways under the houses of Vieux Lyon and Pentes de Croix-Rousse. There are over a 100 in the city, but most of them are closed. The Longue Traboule is the longest and this one is always open. You can find it at 54 Rue Saint-Jean, the main street of Vieux Lyon. Just push the door open and walk all the way through to Rue du Boeuf. This one is kept open for the tourists and in return, the city provides the cleaning of the Traboule, free of charge for the inhabitants of the houses around and above it.

These passageways were used as streets by people in the Middle Ages. They were shortcuts to get to the river quickly. The river was were the poor would get their water. Also, the Traboules were used by the silk workers, who also needed access to water.

The word Traboule comes from latin; trans ambulare, which means walk through.

If you want to find more, they are indicated on the city map from the tourist office (on Place Bellecour). On the map, you will see orange lines between the streets. These are the traboules. To get inside, often, you have to press the service button, which will open the door. Most traboules only open in the morning, to let the postman in.

La Tour Rose

This pretty tower is just an outside staircase. Notice the typical open windows, something you see everywhere in Vieux Lyon. You can find La Tour Rose in the little traboule at 16 Rue du Boeuf. There is a little courtyard here with a shop that sells beautiful pictures.

Just outside, on Rue du Boeuf, there is the famous silk shop 'Maison Brochier'. If you pass by during the silk season, you will see the silk worms crawling outside on a little table. You might also see some moths in a little container. Go inside to find out more about the Silk industry in Lyon. For a little fee, they give you the whole explanation.

Musées Gadagne

You can find this museum at 1, place du Petit-Collège. The museum is about the history of Lyon and there is also a puppet museum. It is only interesting if you want to dig deeper into the history of the city, but not the first museum I would visit. Better to go to the Musée des Beaux-Arts or the Confluence museum. However, don't miss the courtyard. You can go in for free and have a look at this beautiful courtyard. The house belonged to the Italian trading family Gadagni, that frenchified their name to Gadagne. It clearly shows off the wealth you could amass by trading. It was an enormous house.

If it's a nice day and you are looking for a coffee break, just take the elevator to the 4th floor (without paying an entrance ticket). Here, you find a bar and a large roof garden.

Palais de Justice

During the middle ages, this was the residence of the counts of Forez. After, in the renaissance, this was called the Palace of the Kings. The court resided here sometimes. This Palace was destroyed and rebuilt in the 19th century by the architect Baltard, who also designed the Halles de Paris, the central market of Paris. His first idea was to build it on an artificial island in the Saône River, but this was scrapped because of budget constraints.

There are twenty four columns. They should represent the twenty four elders of the apocalypse.

Behind the columns, on the walls, you can see the repeated motive of the Fasces. Fasces are a bundle of sticks, bound together with an axe in the middle. Magistrates in the Roman republic would have people carrying these fasces walking in front of them. The bundled sticks symbolize the power of many. One stick is easy to break, but if you bundle them together, they cannot be broken. The ax symbolized the power over life and death that a magistrate would hold.

In the 19th century, governments loved to put this symbol on their public buildings. You can find a lot of Fasces in the United States, for example inside the Oval Office or on Lincoln's Memorial.

Now, they have a bit of a bad connotation. Italian dictator Mussolini used the symbol for his movement, the movement that he called Fascism.

Now, the Palais de Justice is the Cour d'Assises, the Court of Appeal. The lower court was moved to the Part Dieu area, where now the main train station is located.

If the main door is open, you can have a peek inside the main hall, which is very impressive.

The most famous trial that took place in this building was the trial of Klaus Barbie. Klaus Barbie was the leader of the Gestapo during the Second World War. He was sent to Lyon in 1942, when the Nazi regime wanted to assert a more direct control over Vichy France. He personally tortured many people, including Jean Moulin, the leader of the resistance. Jean died because of the wounds sustained during his interrogation.

Barbie also sent many Jewish orphans down to concentration camps. After the war, he managed to escape. He built a new life for himself in Boliva, as Klaus Altman. He was found there by the French/German Nazi-hunting couple Serge and Beate Klarsfeld. He was extradited to Lyon and convicted to life in prison 1987. He died in prison in the 1990s, still holding on to his Nazi beliefs until the end.

Rue Des Trois Maries

This street is named after the three Maries. This comes from a Provençal legend. According to this legend, the three Maries, Mary Salome (the mother of Saint James), Mary Jacobé (the sister of Mary, Jesus' mother) and Mary Magdalene sailed to the Provence after Jesus' death, where they arrived at Saintes-Maries-de-la-Mer in the Camargue. This is where the Rhone flows into the Mediterranean Sea. Mary Magdalena is even supposed to be buried at Saint Baume in the Provence.

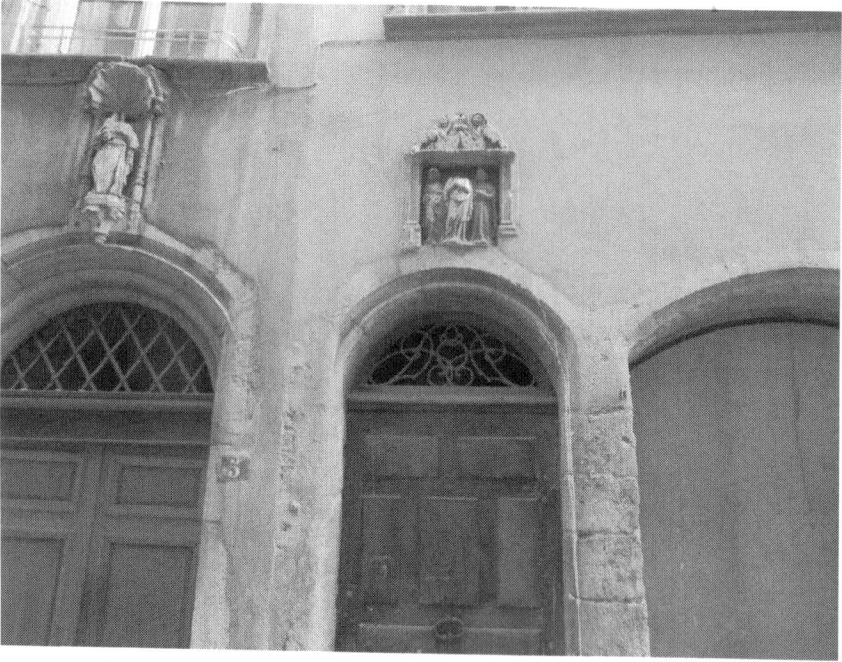

At number seven of this street, you can see a small, broken statue of the three Mary's. When you are here, also have a look up. The building is really nice with windows in four parts and a little ledge that people used to lean out of the window.

There is also a beautiful traboule that leads from this street back to rue St. Jean. You can find it at number 6 of Rue des Trois Maries. You have to press the doorbell and push the very heavy door at the same time. I find this the most beautiful of all the traboules in Vieux Lyon.

Many doors in this street are actually traboules, especially the doors on the eastern side of the street. Until midday, the service button opens a lot of them.

Place de la Baleine

Baleine means whale in French, so this is whale square. You can see a depiction of a whale in wood when you come out of the Rue Des trois Maries. It's on the corner with the Rue de la Baleine.

On this square, big trade fairs were held, which brought enormous prosperity to the city. Florentine bankers made Lyon rich.

On the corner of the square you can see a very popular ice cream shop. It is one of the best in Lyon. They make their own ice cream and even have exotic flavors like tomato and basil.

Place du Gouvernement

All buildings on this square have four floors and they are all different. Have a look at the funny tower with two parallel doors. It's a beautiful square with a tree in the middle. In the middle ages, this was the place where people were executed. The most famous building here is the Hôtel du Gouvernement.

Hôtel du Gouvernement

This building in the corner of the square dates from the end of the 15th century. It was here that the representative of the King lived. He was the 'gouverneur' that was appointed by the king himself. Some kings even stayed in this building when they visited the city. Look at the (mostly broken) small statues on the facade.

You can enter the building and have a look at the nice Traboule.

When you enter, go up the stairs and have a look at the nice and small courtyard. Now, underneath there is a Hookah bar/lounge, but before, these were the stables where people left their horses.

You could even continue down the other stairs to the other side of the building and end up at the river banks. But once you go out from the Traboule, you cannot get back in without knowing the access code.

Place du change

On this square, the most important parts of the medieval fairs were held. Even now, this is the place where open air spectacles are being held in summer. During the middle ages, this was the place where you could change your money. Big tables where set up on the square where bankers conducted their business.

The city became very rich in the sixteenth century and some Italian bankers and cloth merchants came to live here. They often constructed sumptuous houses for themselves.

Because the open air money changing was not very convenient, at some point the 'Loge du Change' was constructed. This is the main building on the square. At the time, it was the only building with its four facades showing. You can completely walk around it without running into other houses.

After the French revolution, the banking business moved to the other bank of the Saône, to the Presqu'Île. This building was converted into a Protestant church. Now the building is called the Temple du Change.

La Maison Thomassin

This is one of the oldest houses in Lyon that are still standing. It was built in the 13th century in Gothic style. Look at the pointed arches of the windows and you can clearly recognize the gothic style.

The building was redone in the 15th century my monsieur Thomassin, who was part of one of the most important families of that time. The Thomassin family had become rich by trading cloth.

The clothing business has always brought prosperity to Lyon. It was King François I who gave the city the privilege to start the clothing industry. Lyon quickly became the number one city in France for the production of fine textile.

Press the doorbell of the small door to the right of the façade of Maison Thomassin to get into a very small courtyard that is beautifully painted in red.

Rue Juiverie

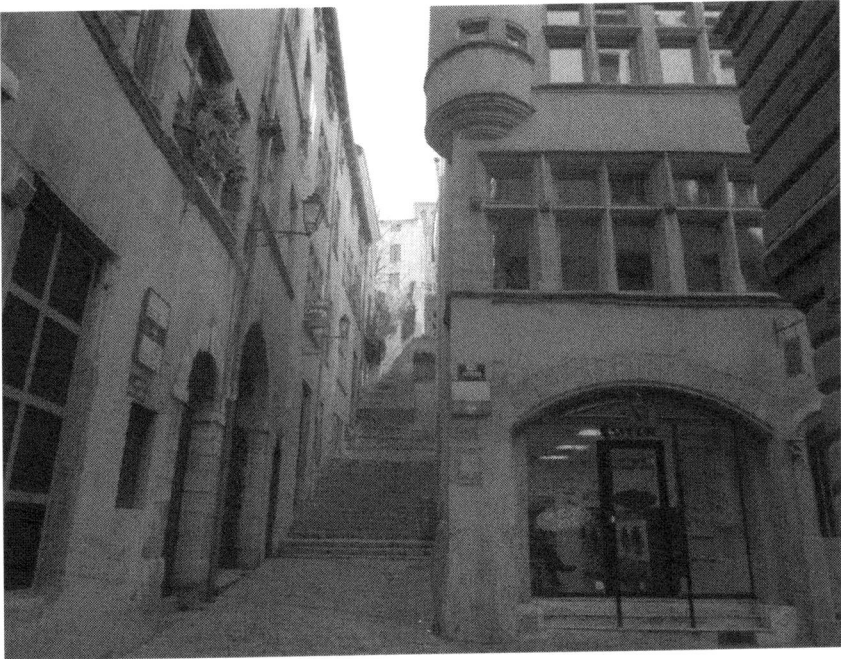

The name of this street still reminds us of the Jewish families that used to live here until they were expelled from the city in the fourteenth century. Look at the facades of the buildings. You can see some funny looking Gargoyles.

In this beautiful street you find many sculptors, theatre associations and artisans. At number 20 there is a famous watch maker. He named his shop after a famous French movie that was shot in these streets: 'L'Horloger de Saint Paul'.

At number 8 there is a famous building, the Hôtel Bullioud. If you can go in, please do. The courtyard is very beautiful. There is a sixteenth century gallery, that was clearly inspired by the Italian Renaissance. It was constructed by famous architect Philibert Delorme, who travelled to Italy to learn the new style of the renaissance. After he created this beautiful gallery in Hôtel Bullioud, he worked on the Fontainebleau palace for the French kings.

The architect Philibert Delorme of the famous Fontainebleau castle designed it after he traveled to Italy. The idea was to connect two parts of the house together by this sort of Loggia. It looks very nice.

Maison Henry IV

This house is named after Henry IV, because he stayed the night here once. It does not look very impressive when you walk passed it on Rue Juiverie, but turn left at the end of the street and walk up. Just around the corner you can see the impressive staircase of the building with a bust of the famous king as extra ornamentation.

The other stairs you see leading up the mountain are called 'La Monté des Carmes Dechaussees'. It used to lead up to a monastery where the nuns used to walk barefeet. 'Dechaussee' means barefoot. You can walk up the stairway just a little, to see the amazing viewpoint just behind the train station. You have a nice view of the Saint-Paul church and the Croix-Rousse hill behind it.

Église de Saint-Paul

If you continue across the square, passed the train station of Saint-Paul, you can already see a small church a bit ahead. It's worth a small detour. It is the Église de Saint-Paul, that has stood here since the 6th century ad. It has a very long building history. Most of the church is a mix of Gothic and Romanesque style. Restorations and additions to the church took place until the 19th century. Have a look inside to admire the beautiful stained glass windows. In the apse, behind the altar, there is a nice fresco of Saint Paul falling off his horse after Jesus miraculously appeared in front of him. This was the moment Saint Paul decided to convert to Christianity.

3. Presqu'île

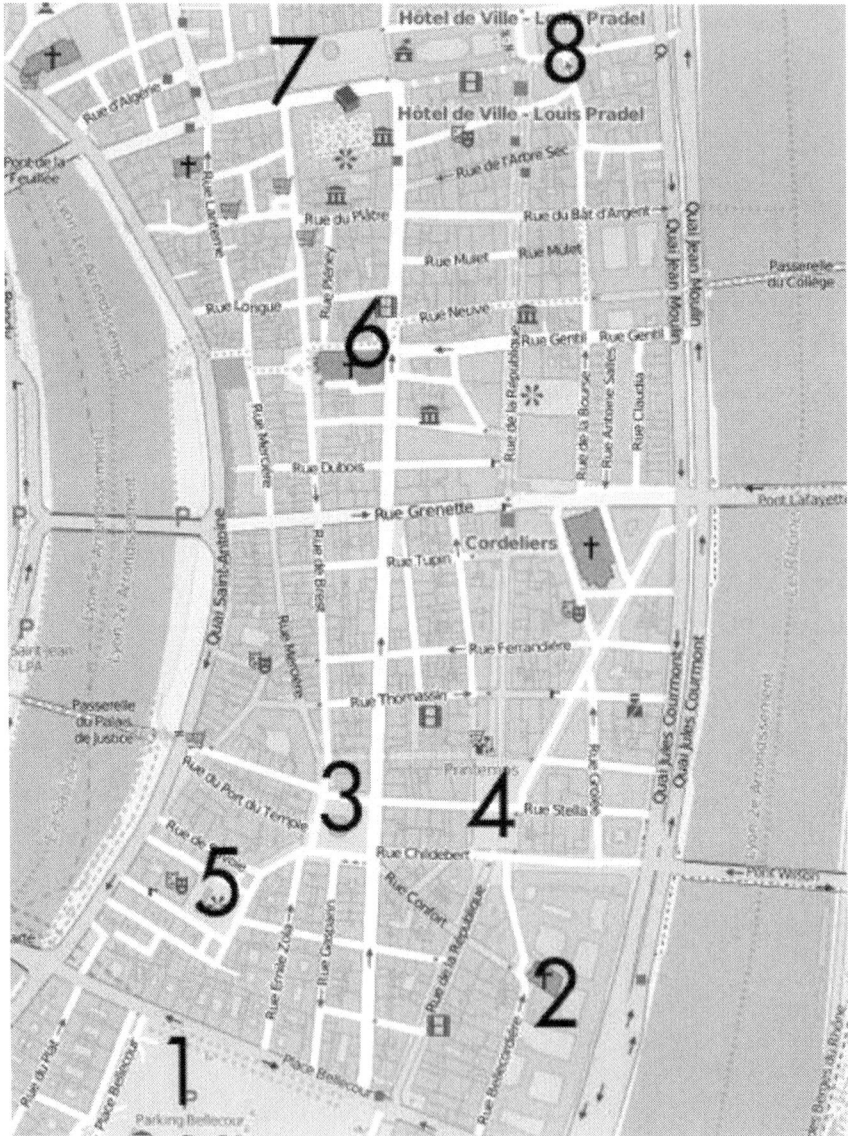

1. Place Bellecour
2. Hôtel-Dieu
3. Place des Jacobins
4. Rue de la République
5. Theatre des Celestins
6. Saint-Nizier
7. Place des Terreaux
8. Opéra Nouvel

Bellecour

Bellecour is a square from the 17th century. It is six hectares big. It was considered the symbol of the ancient regime, so it was destroyed during the French revolution. It was the only square in France that was destroyed in the revolution (1789).

Bellecour is one of the largest open squares in Europe (without greenery or trees) and the 3rd largest in France and the largest pedestrian square in Europe.

Bellecour is km 0 of Lyon. All distances to Lyon are counted from here.

In the early Roman period, this was an island and during the later Roman Empire, there were huts that served as warehouses for boat traders here. In the 12th century, there was a vineyard here that belonged to the archbishop of Lyon, the Bella Curtis (nice garden).

This part of the city consisted mostly of small islands between the two rivers. There were some monasteries here, such as de Benedictine abbey of Ainey

The actual city was located on the other side of the river.

In 1708, Louis XIV became the owner of this land. It was called the Place Royale. A statue of the king was erected here. During the revolution, the square was renamed Place de la Fédération and a guillotine was installed here. The royal statue was destroyed to make a cannon.

After the revolution, it was reconstructed under Napoleon. Eastern and Western facades look a lot alike. They are in neoclassical style, the preferred architectural style of the Empire. Napoleon saw himself as a new Roman Emperor. This was reflected in the art of this period. Architects and sculptors went back to classical examples. The excesses of the baroque and rococo styles were compared to the excesses of the ancient regime. The new style, neoclassicism was much simpler, based on Roman examples. Rococo was the style under Louis XV and XVI.

The Eastern facade occupies 10 blocks of houses and is 150m long.

Louis XIV

The statue of Louis XIV in the middle of the square is in antique style. It was sculpted in 1825 by François-Frédéric Lemot in Paris. The statue is in antique style. If you look, you can see the king is not supported by bristles. This was the way the old emperors of Rome used to be depicted. There is a famous statue of Marcus Aurelius in Rome, where the emperor sits exactly the same way. This way of depicting kings shows them in control. They are quiet on the horse and control it without moving, just like they would control their empire.

Under this statue, you can see two statues, one of the Rhone River and one of the Saône River. The bearded, masculine statue represents the Rhone. Look at the Lion on which he rests. It is the symbol of Lyon.

There is also a statue of Antoine de Saint-Exupéry that was erected in 2000 for the centenary of the writer and aviators birth. He is most famous for writing the book 'the little prince'. You can find the statue at the south-western part of the square, in summer often kind of hidden behind the leaves of the trees.

Place Antonin Poncet

This square is named after a surgeon that used to work in the Hôtel Dieu, just around the corner. The Bell Tower that you can see here standing by itself, used to be the bell tower of the Charity Hospital. This was the second hospital of Lyon, after Hôtel Dieu. It was built in 1622 and destroyed in 1934 to make place for the Post Office. This is the enormous building on the South side of the Square. If it's open, go have a look inside the Post Office, where they have some nice murals, depicting post being delivered all over the world.

Rue de la Barre

This street, that goes from the Guillotière bridge to Bellecour is named after a barrier that used to be here in the Middle Ages. Goods used to come from the other side of the Rhône and were taxed here, before they could come into the city.

Hôtel Dieu

This enormous building, that is currently being repurposed, used to be the most important hospital of the city, but it's history dates back to long before that.

It was built in the 12th century and used to house the urban poor and sick travelers. It was enlarged in the 17th century with the two towers and in the 19th century with the dome and the monumental façade on the side of the Rhône. It has recently re-opened. It's not a hospital anymore, but a shopping center, luxury hotel and conference center. It's nice to hop inside when you're there and have a look at the mix of old an new architecture.

Theatre des Celestins

This theatre was built in 1877. Unfortunately, it burned down completely a few years later, but it was decided to rebuilt it exactly the same. This happened in 1881. It is a beautiful theatre with an impressive façade. The machinery inside is still the same that was used in the 19th century.

In the beginning of the 20th century, this became the second comedy theatre of France, after the Comedié de Paris. Before, there used to be a Celestine monastery here. That is where the name of the theater comes from.

If you are standing in front of the theatre, on the lovely 'Place des Celestins', you might notice a funny looking periscope in the middle of the square. If you look through it, you can see down to the parking lot. It is hard to see sometimes, but the parking lot is quite beautiful. It was designed by architect Michel Targe and the artist Daniel Buren. On the right side of the façade, there are some stairs that lead down to the parking lot. Go ahead and have a look. The parking attendants always show you where to look down into the helical parking space with the turning mirror at the bottom.

Rue de la République

This street is now Lyon's most busy shopping street. Most of it is for pedestrians only. Before the French revolution, this area was filled with small streets and slums. In Paris, the famous architect and city planner Haussmann, devised a plan to get rid of all the small streets. This was to make sure that a new revolution would be much harder to accomplish. He broadened many streets and create the big squares and avenues for which Paris is now famous. This was to make sure the army could easily control groups of people, if they decided to rise up against the authorities.

In Lyon, prefect Vaïsse started a city renovation project that was based on the ideas of Haussmann. Slums were destroyed and big, broad streets and squares where created in the Presqu'île. Rue de la République is the main example of this city renovation project.

The plan worked really well. Rue de la République became the center of Bourgeois Lyon. Sumptuous buildings were occupied by the affluent classes of Lyon.

When you walk down this street, don't forget to look up at the many beautiful buildings. On the ground floor you just see the normal chain stores of any European city, but some floors up you can see beautiful facades and decorations.

Place des Jacobins

This square took its current form during the renovations of prefect Vaïsse. The name of the square comes from the Jacobins, religious preachers from the Dominican order, who owned a convent on the southern side of the square. The fountain in the middle has four statues of famous artists from Lyon. They are: Jean-Hippolyte Flandrin, Gérard Audran, Guillaume Coustou and Philibert Delorme. You might remember the last one as the architect of Fontainebleau castle and the creator of the beautiful loge in the courtyard of the Hôtel Bullioud in Vieux Lyon.

Look at the buildings surrounding the square. They are beautiful and very expensive to live in. All were built in the 1850s.

La Place des Terreaux

This is the main square of Lyon. Here you can find the Hôtel de Ville (city hall) and the Museum of Fine Arts.

In Roman times, there was only a swamp here. It was just a muddy terrain with lots of long ditches across it. This is where the name comes from Terreau is a Medieval word which means something like mud. In the Middle Ages this place became the training ground for soldiers. After, a pig market settled here. It must have looked quite different from today. Imagine a large open unpaved square filled with mud and pigs.

Slowly, this changed. The square was paved and slowly turned into the beautiful square you see now. For a while, public executions took place here.

As the city became richer, the square became nicer. In the 18th century, fancy cafés were opened catered to a rich and bourgeois clientele. Shops were opened and Terreaux became the place it is today.

During the 19th century, the square finally took its current form. Big renovations took place. This was, for example, the time when the gracious fountain was installed on the square. It was created by Bartholdi, the same sculptor that created the statue of liberty in New York. Originally, it was meant for the city of Bordeaux. It was deemed too expensive by Bordeaux. The statue was shown at the World Exposition of Paris in 1889 and after erected in this place. Still, you can see references to Bordeaux in the statue. The water symbolizes the Garonne and its four tributaries, flowing towards the sea.

Hôtel de Ville

This city hall is more than 400 years old. It occupies a large space. When you walk towards the Opera after, you will see how big it is. Look at the impressive bell tower of the Hôtel de Ville. There are four clocks inside, three of which are original from the 17th century. There is also one of the biggest carillons of Europe inside this tower.

The Hôtel de Ville was constructed under Louis XIII and was supposed to be even more impressive than the one in Paris. It took 26 years to build. Some of the building was destroyed by an enormous fire and it was reconstructed under Louis XIV.

During the French Revolution in 1789, the revolutionary tribunal was established here.

Musée des Beaux-Arts

This building used to be a Benedictine Monastery, which dates back to the 7th century A.D. It was reserved for the daughters of the nobility and directed by abbess that was appointed by the king. It was named 'l'Abbaye des Dames de Saint Pierre'. It was a very rich and opulent monastery. The current building was constructed at the same time of the Hôtel de Ville, during the 17th century.

During the revolution, the inhabitants of the monastery were thrown out and under Napoleon the building became a museum. It has a really impressive collection of art. You can find art from all periods here, from Egyptian artifacts to paintings by Picasso and Monet. It is well worth a visit. Even if you don't have time or are not an art lover, enter through the main gate of the building, to admire the beautiful green courtyard.

In spring and summer the benches here are filled with people eating lunch and chatting quietly. It's a lovely retreat from a busy city, which makes sense, because it used to be the courtyard of the convent, which also served the purpose of providing a quiet retreat for the nuns.

L'Opéra de Lyon

This Opera house has been standing here for two centuries now. It was built in the beginning of the 19th century, but it has been renovated many times, something which is quite obvious when you look at the building. You can already see the strange mixture between the neoclassical façade and the modern architecture of the vault shaped roof. This is the result of a contest that was held at the end of the 20th century. The opera had to be enlarged and renovated and the architect with the best idea got to do the renovations.

In the end, it was the famous architect Jean Nouvel that won this contest and the building you see today is a product of his imagination. He only kept the neoclassical façade of the building and the sumptuous salon at the first floor (which you can already admire from the outside). He then constructed a modern opera house inside this old façade. He enlarged it by envisioning an enormous rounded vault that towered above the old building. I quite like this mix of old and modern, but it is not for everybody.

To admire the amazing view from the top, at night (Wednesday until Saturday), you can have a drink at the bar behind the muses (the big statues on top). The elevator to the bar is outside.

Saint-Nizier

This is one of my favorite churches in Lyon. I think its interior is of a simple beauty that many other churches in Lyon lack. So, if you pass by, make sure to go inside, even if it's just for a minute. The outside façade does not impress me that much, but the inside is simply beautiful, even though it is sparsely decorated.

Before there was a church here, it is believed that there was a Roman Temple. This you can see often in cities with a Roman past. With the advent of Christianity, churches had to be built and what better place to build them, than right on top of the temples of the old gods, who only heathens would worship.

It is believed that there was a temple of Attis, the Phrygian god of vegetation, here. In the fifth century, a church was built here. So this was a really early church. You must already see that the current building is not from the fifth century. The structure you see now has been built from the 14th century until the 16th century. It has a clear gothic style. Can you see the pointed arches everywhere in the architecture?

4. Pentes de Croix Rousse

This area lies on the hill north of Place des Terreaux. It is an interesting area, with lots of vintage shops, small restaurants and bars. It is nice to walk up all the way, to enjoy the view at the top of the hill. There is a pedestrian walkway (Montée de la Grande-Côte) that leads all the way up, with many cool shops and bars along the way.

This area is also famous for the many traboules. You can find them by looking for the tiny signs on the walls. Often, you will see a little sign of an arrow and an eye. If you follow the sign, you end up in a traboule that will lead you up or down the hill.

The Cour des Voraces

The Cour des Voraces is one of the most famous traboules in Lyon. You can find it at Place Colbert 9 and it leads to Rue Imbert-Colomès or the Montée de Saint-Sébastien 14b (it has two exits). The courtyard of the traboule is famous for the monumental staircase.

The vorace were an informal association of silk workers that gathered here to fight for better working conditions. They were among the instigators of various uprisings of the Canuts (silk workers) during the 19th century. They even feature in books by Karl Marx, who saw these uprisings as a first example of the progression from industry to revolution.

The Roman Amphitheatre

The main tourist attraction on this hill is the Roman Amphitheater. What is an Amphitheater? You get an amphitheater when you put two theaters together. This way, you get an arena, just like the colosseum. Here, the Romans organized gladiator fights and hunting games. The amphitheater was built in 19 A.D. and expanded in the second century. 20.000 people could be seated here.

Now, not much is left to see. You cannot enter the site, but you can see most of it from the outside. If you have to choose between visiting the Roman Theatre on Fourvière hill or this Amphitheatre, visit the Theater. That site is much more impressive.

The amphitheater is infamous in the history of Lyon, because in 177 A.D., many of the early Christians of the city were put to death here during a persecution under emperor Marcus Aurelius. According to legend, at midnight you can still hear the screaming of the martyrs around the amphitheater.

La Maison des Canuts

If you are interested in the history of silk production of Lyon, you can visit the Maison des Canuts on the Croix Rousse hill. You find it at 10-12, rue d'Ivry. Here, you will learn everything about the production process and the cultivation of silk worms. Visit the website (http://www.maisondescanuts.fr/) for opening times and reservations for guided tours.

Marché Alimentaire de la Croix-Rousse

This market, on the Boulevard de la Croix-Rousse is one of the nicest produce markets in the city. It is open all days until 12:00 except Mondays. Wednesday and Thursday it is a lot smaller. It's a great place to admire all the lovely produce that the countryside around town produces. You can buy great cheeses, admire beautiful vegetables and look at the so-called *triperie*, the intestines that feature so prominently in the cuisine of the city.

5. Fourvière

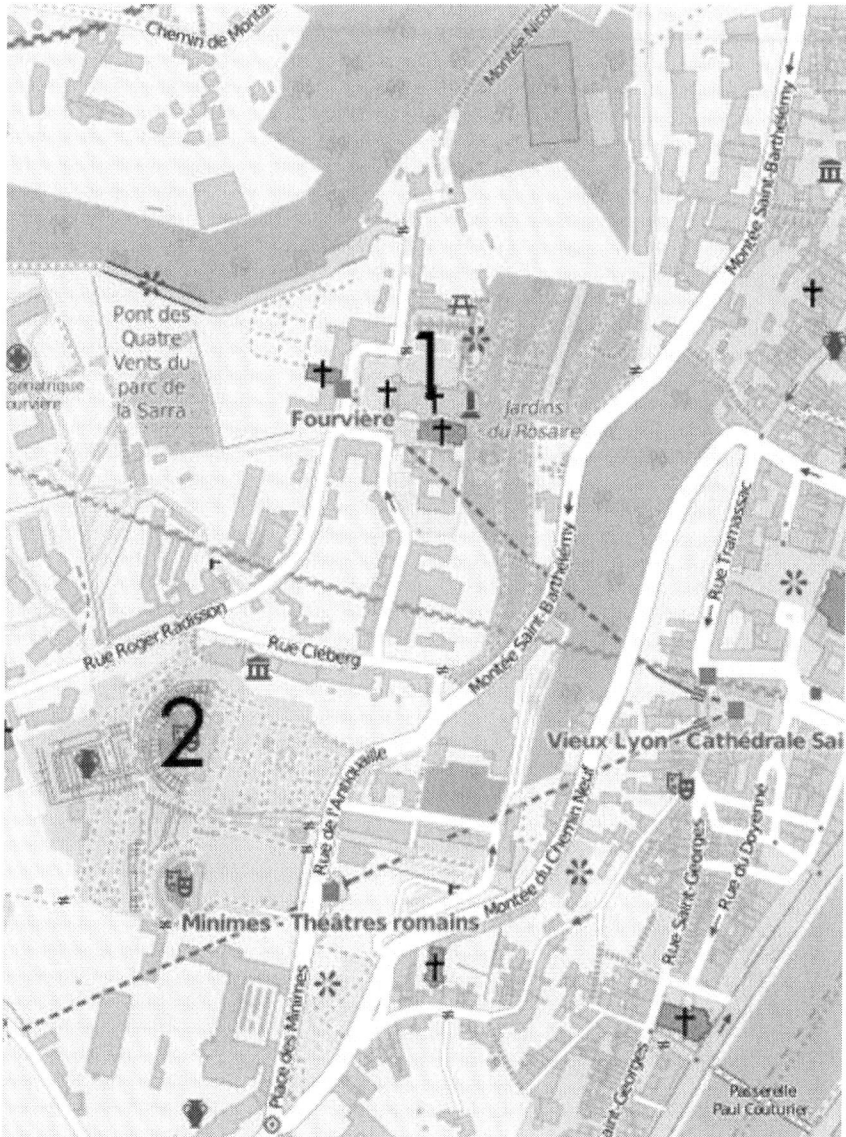

1. Notre-Dame de Fourvière
2. Roman Theatre

Basilica of Notre-Dame de Fourvière

This church towers high above the city and is one of the highlights of a visit to Lyon. Long before there was any church on this place, it used to be the main square of the city. This was when the Romans still ruled over Lyon. In fact, the name Fourvière comes from the Latin word Forum Vetus, or Old Forum. This was the forum, or market square, that was built under emperor Trajan. Later, the Latin Forum Vetus was slowly Frenchified to Fourvière.

Ever since the 17th century, there used to be a chapel here that was dedicated to the Virgin Mary. It was believed that the Virgin had protected Lyon from the Bubonic plague in 1643. During this time, many people died in many cities, but not in Lyon. So to thank Mary for her protection, a chapel was built on this hill. The people from Lyon still commemorate this miracle every 8th of December, during the Festival of Light. Now, this *Fête des Lumières* is one of the main tourist attractions of the city. Many people flock to Lyon to see the buildings of the city richly decorated with lights and projections.

This church was built to commemorate another miracle. In 1870, the Prussians invaded France and wreaked havoc all around the country. Fortunately for Lyon, the city was spared an invasion. This was also attributed to the protection the city always received from the Virgin Mary. To thank her, the Basilica de Notre-Dame de Fourvière was built with private money.

So, the church is a lot newer than the Cathedral Saint-Jean down in Vieux Lyon. The style of architecture of the building is very eclectic. The architect, Pierre Bossan, was influenced a lot by the styles of the churches in Palermo in Sicily. He had just visited the city and came back impressed by the beautiful churches that the Norman kings had built when they ruled over Sicily. These churches, like the Capella Palatina and the Duomo of Monreale also blend a lot of styles. The Normans used Arab and Byzantine workmen to decorate French Romanesque churches.

Fourvière is clearly inspired by these buildings in Palermo, especially when you go inside. The church is richly decorated with mosaics, that almost look byzantine. In them, you can see stories from the history of the church in France.

When you go in, do not forget to visit the lower church. There are actually two churches built on top of each other. The lower church is easily missed if you don't know it exists. You can get to it by taking the door on the right side in the middle of the church and going down the stairs. You will get to the lower basilica, on top of which the main church is built.

Local residents call the church an upside-down elephant. The four towers are the legs of the elephant.

When you are up here, make sure to have a look at the view, from the square next to the church. From here, you have a beautiful view over Vieux Lyon, Presqu'île and sometimes you can even look as far as the Mont Blanc.

To reach the church, most people take the funiculaire, which can be accessed from the Vieux Lyon metro stop.

The Roman Theater

If you visit Fourvière hill, make sure to have a look at the Roman Theatre. The site is for free and there is a nice park around it. The theatre was built by the Romans and the sheer size of it can give you an idea of how big this city actually was.

At its high point, Lyon was the second most important city in the Western Roman Empire, after Rome itself. The first little theatre was built on this site in 15 BC. In the beginning of the second century AD, it was expanded and could house 10.000 people.

In the summer, a music festival takes place here, the *Nuits de Fourvière*. International acts like Radiohead and Norah Jones played here.

Musée Gallo-Romain

If you are interested in the Roman history of the city, visit this museum at 17, rue Cléberg. It is located above the Roman Theatres and the building itself is also interesting. It was designed by architect Bernard Zehrfuss.

Because Lyon was the capital of Gaul during the Roman empire, archeologists still find many interesting objects all around the city, which inevitably end up in this museum.

6. Confluence and Other Interesting Places

The Musée des Confluences

This is a very new museum. Confluence is the area where the two rivers join. The Saône joins the Rhône and continues down south to the Mediterranean Sea. This area used to be very run down. There was an old port here and prostitution and drug dealing were rampant. A few years back, the city decided to clean up the whole area.

Now this is a showcase for modern architecture. I find it really fun to walk around the area, especially around the Saône side. Take the tram T1 from Perache station to Debourg and get off at the big modern shopping center (a lot of people will get off here). Have a coffee at the top floor of this futuristic shopping center or walk down to the Saône and go downriver to the exact point where the two rivers come together. You can find futuristic offices, like the apple green headquarters of Euronews, residences that look like blue spaceships and the impressive Musée des Confluences.

This museum was designed by the famous Austrian architects of the Coop-Himmelblau studio. It is supposed to look like a floating crystal cloud of steel and glass. It is certainly an impressive building. It stands right on the spot where the two rivers come together. It is a science museum and I always enjoy visiting it. The expositions are always very well done.

If you decide to skip it, make sure to enter the building, just to take the elevator to the top floor. Here you can enjoy the view and the building for free and have a cup of coffee in the bar of the museum.

Parc de la Tête d'Or

You can find this park on the riverbanks of the Rhône. It is the biggest public park in the center of Lyon and lovely to visit on a nice day. Many Lyonnais go here on Saturdays and Sundays to enjoy the green spaces. There is a free zoo, so don't be surprised if you see giraffes walking around all of a sudden.

Another nice thing to visit here is the Botanical Garden (also for free). If you see the big greenhouses from the 19th century, just open the door and enjoy the tropics for a while. Many of the plants here come from the former French colonies.

Inside the big lake in the middle there is a small island. You can access it by going through a tunnel on the west side of the lake. On the island there is a monument to the many soldiers that died during the wars of the 20th century.

Cité Internationale

Locked in between the Rhône and the Park de la Tête d'Or are the very modern buildings of the Cité Internationale. It is fun to walk around if you like modern architecture. There is a big congress center here and many offices. You also find many enormous and often funny colorful statues. There are also some places to have lunch here.

7. Restaurants

Lyon is called the culinary capital of France. It has one of the highest ratios of restaurants per capita in Europe. Lyon got this title because it has always been a central place, where amazing ingredients from the countryside are easy to find. Here you find a list of ten amazing restaurants that are very popular by locals, but I encourage you to search online as well. One of the best sites to find great restaurants is the website of the Michelin guide (https://restaurant.michelin.fr/restaurants/lyon).

Obviously, the starred restaurants are not always in everybody's price range, but you can search for the restaurants with the Bib Gourmand. These are restaurants that have 'normal' prices, but still well worth checking out. The website also offers lunch and dinner deals.

List of amazing local restaurants

Make sure to call beforehand to make a reservation. These places are very popular.

Le Kitchen Café
34 rue Chevreul, + 33 6 03 36 42 75, lekitchencafe.com.
Open Weds-Sun 8.30am-6-3pm

Café Sillon
46 avenue Jean Jaurès, +33 4 78 72 09 73, cafe-sillon.com. Tues-Sat (closed Sat lunch)

Bouchon Thomas
1,3,6,8, rue Laurencin, +33 4 72 60 94 53, restaurant-thomas.com.
Mon-Fri lunch and dinner

Burgundy Lounge
24 quai Sainte-Antoine, +33 4 72 04 04 51, burgundylounge.fr. Open seven days a week, lunch Mon-Fri, tasting menu only Sat eve).

Les Apothicaires
23 rue de Sèze +33 4 26 02 25 09, lesapothicairesrestaurant.com.
Mon-Fri lunch and dinner

Les Trois Dômes
20 quai Gailleton, +33 4 72 41 20 97, les-3-domes.com. Tues-Dat
lunch and dinner

Le Garet
7 rue du Garet, +33 4 78 28 16 94, no website. Mon-Fri lunch and
dinner

Le Café du Peintre
50 boulevard de Brotteaux, +33 78 52 52 61, lecafedupeintre.com.
Mon-Fri lunch, Thur-Friday dinner

L'Ébauche
4 rue de la Martinière, +33 4 78 58 12 58, on Facebook. Weds(dinner
only)-Sun

Le Potager des Halles
3 rue de la Martinière, +33 4 72 00 24 84, lepotagerdeshalles.com.
Tues-Sat lunch and dinner

If you really like high quality food, you could also visit the Halles Paul
Bocuse, named after the famous chef. The building is not really nice
(looks like a concrete parking garage), but you can get some really
great food here. It looks like a market, but the prices (and quality) are
much higher. You can find it close to the Part-Dieu train station at
102 Cours Lafayette.

8. Museums in Lyon

Confluence Museum

The confluence museum is the new science museum. It has a lovely fixed exhibition and also organizes temporary exhibitions. Check the website to find out what is going on. The building is a great piece of modern architecture that resembles a space ship.

86 Quai Perrache, 69002 Lyon
+33 4 28 38 12 12
www.museedesconfluences.fr

The Lyon Museum of Fine Arts

The fine art museum houses the biggest art collection in France outside of Paris. There are a lot of paintings from very early middle ages to modern art. The building used to be a monastery and inside the old church you find a lovely collection of statues. Also worth it to just go inside and have a look at the courtyard.

20 Place des Terreaux, 69001 Lyon
+33 4 72 10 17 40
www.mba-lyon.fr

Movies & Miniature Museum

This is a very funny museum. It houses a collection of miniatures and also costumes and artifacts from Hollywood movies. You can spend easily hours here and not be bored. It is not the Louvre, but it is fun.

60 Rue Saint-Jean, 69005 Lyon
+33 4 72 00 24 77
www.museeminiatureetcinema.fr

Gallo-Roman Museum of Lyon-Fourvière

This museum houses all the finds from ancient Lugdunum, when Lyon was the capital of France under the Romans. It is located next to the Roman Theater, which you can visit for free.

17 Rue Cleberg, 69005 Lyon
+33 4 72 38 49 30
www.museegalloromain.grandlyon.com

Musées Gadagne

This is the local history museum. It is not the first museum I would visit in Lyon, unless you like old maps and paintings of the city from bygone times. There is a lovely, hidden, roof garden with bar on top, that you can visit without paying entrance fee to the museum.

1 Place du Petit Collège, 69005 Lyon
+33 4 78 42 03 61
www.gadagne.musees.lyon.fr

Museum of Printing and Graphic Communication

This is the print museum, which can be nice to visit for graphic designers or people that have an interest in fonts and printing presses.

13 Rue de la Poulaillerie, 69002 Lyon
+33 4 78 37 65 98
www.imprimerie.lyon.fr

Centre d'histoire de la Résistance et de la Déportation

This is the Resistance Museum, housed in the old headquarters of the Gestapo. It is an interesting museum, but less so if you don't read or speak French. No translations!

14 Avenue Berthelot, 69007 Lyon
+33 4 72 73 99 00
www.chrd.lyon.fr

Musée Lumière

This museum is housed in the old villa of the Lumière brothers, the inventors of cinema. Visit it if you are interested in the development of early cinema. They also screen movies and organize a Film Festival.

25 Rue du Premier Film, 69008 Lyon
+33 4 78 78 18 95
www.institut-lumiere.org

Tony Garnier Urban Museum

Tony Garnier was a visionary city planner and architect from Lyon. The nicest thing about this museum are the many enormous murals that you can find on the buildings around the museum, outside. If you like street art, this is a funny neighborhood to visit.

4 Rue des Serpollières, 69008 Lyon
+33 4 78 75 16 75
www.museeurbaintonygarnier.com

9. Practical information for your visit

Metro in Lyon

The metro or subway system in Lyon is pretty straightforward. There are four metro lines and two funiculars. A ticket costs a bit less than two euros and is valid on the busses and trams as well. If you buy more than 10 tickets, the price drops. You can also buy daily tickets. Check the website of TCL (the operator of public transport in Lyon) for more information. You find ticket vending machines in all stations as well as maps.

http://www.tcl.fr/en

Busses and trams

Busses and trams in Lyon are part of the metro system. With one ticket, you can change from a bus to a metro and vice versa. There are some nice and modern trolley busses in Lyon that take you anywhere in the city. The tram lines are also very efficient. Modern trams take you to Confluence, the train station and many other parts in the city.

City Bikes

Lyon has an awesome system of city bikes. For less than 2 euro you can get a daily ticket and use the bikes for half an hour at a time. A yearly pass just costs about 30 euros. All throughout Lyon, you find docking station. There is even a smartphone app that shows you where they are and if bikes are available.

https://velov.grandlyon.com/

Taxis in Lyon

There are taxi stops all throughout the city. You can also call taxis, or have someone (from the restaurant or hotel) call a taxi for you. Uber works around the city. There is also a smartphone app and website where you can order taxis in Lyon.

https://www.taxilyon.com/

Airport Transfer

Lyon is connected to the Saint-Exupery Airport with a tram link, the Rhônexpress. It's a very convenient way to get to the city, but relatively expensive (compared to other European cities). The tram stops at metro stop Vaulx-en-Velin - La Soie, from where you can take the subway to Bellecour. If you stay in the tram, it takes you to Part-Dieu, the main train station.

https://www.rhonexpress.fr/

Walking in Lyon

If you are staying around the city center, everything is pretty much in walking distance. Lyon is a very easy city to walk around. The main areas of Vieux Lyon and Presqu'Île are flat and easy to get around. Most of the highlights of Lyon are located pretty close to each other. Some, like the hidden passageways of Vieux Lyon, can only be explored on foot.

Plat du Jour

During the week, most French restaurants offer a cheap day plate, the plat du jour. It's a great way to eat out for a small price.

Many of Lyon's nice restaurants have an inexpensive day plate. Remember, a bottle of tap water should always be provided for free. If not, just ask for a carafe d'eau.

Bouchon

The Bouchon are the traditional restaurants of Lyon. They serve hearty meals in an informal setting. Try some of the classic dishes, such as the quenelle de brochet, tripe a la lyonnaise or andouillete. Better not to look up what these dishes are made from. If you are a vegetarian, better to skip the bouchon.

Tipping

In France, by law, service is always included in the price. However, it is becoming more customary to leave a little tip. You can round up the price of your meal, or leave about 5%. In bars, nobody really tips, but the waiter or barman will surely appreciate the gesture. At a coffee place, it's not customary at all to leave a tip, but you can leave a little change.

Wine

You can obviously get amazing wines in Lyon. Go to a wine store and let the people help you. Tell them your budget, and they will surely come up with an amazing wine. It's also lovely to go to a wine bar. For 5 euros you can get a great glass of wine. Again, ask the barman for some of his favorites and you'll get something special most of the time. Local wines are the Côte du Rhône and the Beaujolais.

Water

You can drink the water from the tap without problems in Lyon. In a restaurant or eatery, they are supposed to serve you free water if you ask for it. This is a law in France. Ask for a carafe d'eau and they will bring you a bottle of tap water. This can save you quite a bit of money.

Michelin

To explore Lyons food culture more extensively, go to the Michelin guidebook website. Here, you find all the starred restaurants and also the Bib Gourmand, the restaurants with the best quality/price ratio.

https://restaurant.michelin.fr/restaurants/lyon/

10. Historic Background

Rome

Lyon was founded 43 before Christ by Lucius Munatius Plancus, who was a lieutenant of Julius Caesar, with veterans from the Gallic wars. Lyon became the Capital of France for the Romans. 50.000 people lived here, which was enormous for that age. The biggest Amphitheater (Colosseum) of Gaul stood in Lyon (the remains can still be seen in the Pentes de Croix-Rousse neighborhood). 20.000 people fit in this arena, where gladiators fought. On the Fourvière hill, you can admire the remains of the Roman theatre, still used to this day, 2000 years after they were built.

Once a year, representatives of all the Gallic tribes had to come to Lyon to pay homage to the emperor, at an altar on the Pentes de Croix-Rousse, close to the Amphitheatre. Archeologists are still looking for this altar, which must be somewhere under the modern houses.

Background

Julius Caesar crossed the alps and conquered Gaul (modern day France). Historians estimate he killed one third of the Gauls, enslaved another third and left the remaining Gauls alone. Many Roman veterans from the war settled in France, on the lands they were given as reward. Julius Caesar returned to Italy, crossed the Rubicon and took power in Rome as a dictator, which ended the Roman Republic.

Emperor Claudius was born in Lyon in 10 before Christ. When he became emperor in 41 A.D., he granted the nobility of Lyon the right to become senators in Rome. Around the Amphitheatre, big bronze plates with his speech were found in the street that is now called Rue des Tables Claudiennes. The plates are now on display in the Musée Gallo-Romain in Lyon.

Early Christianity

The bishop of Lyon is a powerful man in the French Church. He even has a special title: the Primat des Gaules, or the 'first among the Gauls'. This is because the first Christians in France were in Lyon. The first Christian community in France existed here. Lyon has a very direct connection with Christ. Christ had a student called St. John the evangelist, St John had a student called St Polycarpe and St. Polycarpe had a student called St. Irenée. Irenée came to Lyon from Smyrna (current Izmir, Turkey) and became the second bishop of Lyon. Therefore, Lyon has a very direct connection to the teachings of Christ. The writings of Irenaeus of Lyon are still studied by theology students all around the world.

Many early Christians died in the persecutions by the Romans in 177 A.D. under emperor Marcus Aurelius in the Amphitheatre on the Pentes de Croix-Rousse.

Background

Christianity was illegal during the Roman empire until emperor Constantine legalized it in 313 (with his Edict of Milan). Christians were persecuted up until that point because they refused to worship the emperor as a god. Christians only believe in one god. Many died during persecutions. The first one was 64 A.D., under emperor Nero, when Saint Peter and Paul died in Rome, but there were many more. In Lyon, many Christians died in 177 under Emperor Marcus Aurelius. They were thrown in front of wild animals in the Amphitheatre.

The Middle Ages

Lyon only became part of France in 1312. Before, it was part of the Holy Roman Empire. During this period the Cathedral was built (from 1180 until 1480). It is one of the first gothic buildings in

France, after Saint Denis in Paris. In the cathedral Clement V was crowned Pope in 1305. This started what is called the Babylonian captivity of the papacy. For decades, the popes lived in Avignon and not in Rome (1305-1376).

When Clement V was crowned in Lyon, a wall collapsed on the Fourvière hill, because so many people came to look. Many in the crowd died and the pope fell. Apparently, one of the precious stones on the pope's crown fell and was never recovered.

Lyon at this time was located mostly in Vieux Lyon. On Presqu'île, the modern city center between the two rivers, there were a few churches and abbeys (like the beautiful Saint Martin d'Ainay, which still exists), but not much else.

Background

The word gothic is an insult given to this style of architecture by Italian artists of the Renaissance. They did not like the gothic style at all and named it after the Goths. The Ostrogoths and Visigoths had invaded the Roman empire and sacked Rome in 420 A.D. Gothic meant barbaric. The Italians considered this Northern European style a barbaric style of architecture. In fact, in Italy you do not find a lot of gothic architecture.

Why did the pope move to Avignon? Why was the pope crowned in Lyon and not in Rome? This started a while before. Philip IV (le bel or the handsome) spent too much money and decided to tax the church. The pope at the time was called Boniface VIII. He was not happy at all at this. He issued a Papal Bull, Unam Sanctam, which said that the pope stands above Kings because he is the representative of God on earth. Boniface argued that he had the right to depose kings. Understandably, Philip did not agree. He sent his ambassador with some thugs to the home of the pope in the town of Anagni in Italy. There, they slapped him in the face. Italians still remember this as the Schiaffo di Anagni, the slap of Anagni.

The pope was so upset that he died shortly after. Philip managed to influence the college of Cardinals and soon after got a French pope elected, Clement V. Clement didn't live in Rome (he was bishop of Bordeaux) and didn't want to live in Bordeaux. He chose to be crowned in Lyon and moved to Avignon. There is still an enormous papal palace in Avignon. Only in 1420 did a pope move back to Rome.

Renaissance

Lyon was a trading city and had strong connections with Italy. In those days, there was just one bridge over the Saône and only one across the Rhone. People coming from Italy had to pass through Lyon and people going there also had to pass through Lyon. Many traders from Italy settled in Lyon to facilitate trade. A lot of trade was with Florence, which had a strong textile industry at the time, but there was also trade in luxury goods that came from the east through the silk roads through Venice, Genoa and Pisa. Silks from China, spices from Indonesia and India and things like lapis lazuli (blue pigment stone) from Afghanistan all came through the silk roads to Italy and were then sold through Lyon to rich people in France, Germany and Spain.

A lot of Bankers from Lucca, Italy also moved to Lyon, to loan money to the French kings and aristocrats. Still to this day there is a strong banking sector in Lyon (LCL for example).

Lyon got the right from king Charles VIII to hold four trade fairs a year. Caravans of goods came over the alps and from the north and fairs could last a few weeks. On Place du Change, in Vieux Lyon, stands the Maison Thomassin, where now the chocolate shop Voisin is located. The Thomassin family was a trading family from Normandy, that made a lot of money trading with the Italians and were able to buy a big house in Lyon.

Background

During the Renaissance, new ideas came from Italy to France through Lyon. The Italians had rediscovered classical art and used this as an inspiration to improve in many fields. Many French people came into contact with Italian culture through wars and marriage. Charles VIII of France invaded Italy (many see this as the official end of the renaissance in Italy). The French aristocrats that came with him learned to appreciate Italian art and life. Also, French kings started to marry Italian princesses, like Catherine and Marie de Medici. (Henri IV married Marie in the cathedral of Lyon). They became queens of France and were a tremendous influence on French culture. Catharine ate with a fork, which was the custom in Florence at the time. Soon, there were no more medieval banquets during which whole pigs where roasted and eaten by hand. Now, everybody had a knife and fork and dinner became much more civilized at court. Catherine also brought many cooks from Italy with her. This was also a major influence on French cuisine, which became much more refined afterwards.

Artists were also influenced by the Italians. Lyon's greatest architect, Philibert Delorme, moved to Italy to study the architecture of Brunelleschi, Alberti and Michelangelo. He returned to Lyon and designed some of the earliest renaissance architecture in Lyon, for example the well in the courtyard of Maison du Chamarier and the Gallerie Philibert Delorme in the Maison Bullioud in Rue Juiverie. He later became the architect of the court and redesigned the Fontainebleau castle (where the kings spent a lot of time before moving to Versailles) in Renaissance style for Henri II and Catherine de Medici. You can see a statue of Philibert on Place des Jacobins.

Protestants versus Catholics

On 30 April 1562 the protestants of Lyon took control over the city. This lasted a year. The protestants destroyed many of the statues on and inside the cathedral. They were followers of Calvin, the Swiss preacher.

Background

In 1517 Luther nailed his 95 theses on the church door in Wittenberg, starting the protestant revolution. Soon, religious wars swept through Europe. This was not a minor disagreement between Protestants and Catholics, these were vicious wars. The protestants in Lyon were afraid of the catholic majority and took control with the help of a mercenary army of the Baron des Adrets.

Calvin had said that there is only one god. The catholic worship of Saints and Angels was heretic. You should not worship stone statues of saints that are not gods, he thought. Therefore, the protestants destroyed many statues and church decorations wherever they took power. In Holland, all the inside decorations of the former catholic churches and cathedrals were completely destroyed by followers of Calvin. Even now, protestant churches are very sober from the inside.

Silk

In 1536, King François I gave Lyon the right to produce silk. This soon became the major industry of the city, up until the 19th century. Half of the population of Lyon depended on the silk production and trade.

The production was dominated by 300 powerful silk traders, that controlled the silk. They did not possess workshops or looms however. Then, there were about 8000 Maître-ateliers, the owners of the workplaces. Lowest in the pyramid where the 40.000 compagnons that worked in the ateliers, often in horrible working conditions. They often slept right at the atelier of their master.

In 1804, Joseph Marie Jacquard invented the Jacquard loom. This was a very important innovation. Instead of 2 people, now you only needed one person to operate this loom. It worked with punch cards, a big stack of cards that programmed the machine. Some people see this loom as the precursor to computers. The first computers also worked with paper punch cards and to this day, some machines in the textile industry still work with punch cards.

The Jacquard loom might have indirectly led to the uprising of the silk workers (canuts in the local dialect) in 1831. People lost their job because the work could be done by 1 instead of 2.

Now there are only 10 people left in the city that know how to operate a silk loom.

Fourvière

The name of the hill comes from Forum Vetus, old Forum. The romans had left the hill when the aqueducts fell into disrepair. People had to walk down the hill to get water and so the hill was abandoned. The Lyonnais used the Roman remains for centuries as quarries, a place to get cheap stone to build their houses and churches.

The Tour Metallique (the little counterfeit Eiffel Tower) was built by republicans to spite the church. It is higher than the Notre dame de Fourvière.

In 1643, the aldermen (echevins) of Lyon dedicated the city to the virgin, to thank her for saving the city from the plague. There was a little chapel dedicated to the virgin on top of the hill.

The chapel was transformed into the modern church we see now after Mary had saved the city again after 1870, when the Prussians under Bismarck invaded.

Background

During the Franco-Prussian war of 1870 the Prussians invaded France. They laid siege to Paris. The city was surrounded. This was a horrible time for Paris. Food ran out and there are many descriptions of people having to eat cats and dogs. Even all the zoo animals were butchered and sold as meat. Understandably, the Lyonnais were very afraid the war would come to their city, so they promised their protectress, Mary, that they would build a big church in her honor if she stopped the Prussians. The Prussians never came to the city and so to thank the virgin, the Notre Dame de Fourvière was built.

The Prussians won the war and invaded Paris. In Versailles, under Chancellor Bismarck, a treaty was signed that led to the unification of Germany under Prussia. It also led to such unfavorable conditions for France that World War I broke out a few decades later.

Resistance

The Resistance was very strong and powerful in Lyon. Lyon is also called La Capitale de la Resistance. Jean Moulin, the leader of the resistance, had left for London where he met Charles de Gaulle. He got the assignment to come back to France to unify the resistance. He was parachuted into the Provence and made his way to Lyon. Here he lived in different apartments around Place Carnot next to the Perrache train station.

Klaus Barbi was the leader of the Gestapo. The resistance leaders were betrayed and arrested when they met for a meeting in Caluire. Klaus Barbie personally tortured Jean Moulin, who died on a train to Germany from his wounds.

After the war Barbie escaped with help from the CIA, to assist the Americans in their fight against Communism. He became an intelligence officer in Bolivia and enjoyed close contact with some right-wing dictators. Nazi hunters from France found out who he was and after a new democratic government was elected in Bolivia, he was extradited. He stood trial in Lyon in the Cour d'assises and was convicted in 1987. He died four years later in prison.

Capitale de la Gastronomie

Lyon is famous for its food. The countryside around Lyon has always produced great quality produce. The best chicken from France come from Bourg-en-Bresse, every village around seems to produce its own cheese and farms grow all sorts of vegetables. The chefs in Lyon always had a lot to work with. Before the invention of refrigeration, this was important.

Around the end of the 19th century, the bouchon came into existence. Many mothers or aunts, Les Mères and Les Tantes, opened little eateries to make a bit of extra money for their families. Many girls had lost their job, working for rich families and started business by themselves.

A great example is La Mère Brazier. She was a girl from the countryside with a baby. The father was nowhere to be found. She moved to the city and managed to find a job in one of the bouchon. She was so good that she soon opened her own bouchon, which promptly received three Michelin stars. Her second bouchon also received three stars, a feat that nobody has managed to repeat.

Many of the great chefs of Lyon started in her kitchen, like Paul Bocuse. Bocuse later became the first celebrity chef. He was of tremendous importance for Lyon and French Cuisine. He was a major exponent of the Nouvelle Cuisine. Chefs started preparing lighter dishes, with less sauces and new techniques. Salmon was not cooked through and through but got a more Japanese kind of treatment. Bocuse was a star in the 70s and 80s. He cooked for presidents, opened many Brasserie in Lyon (Le Nord, L'Est, Le Sud and L'Oeste). He founded a cooking school, l'Institut Paul Bocuse, where you can do courses for amateurs, but also four year Master courses that cost 18000 euro a year. There is also the upscale food market, Les Halles Paul Bocuse, close to Part Dieu train station. Here you find the best food the city has to offer and outside, you find an enormous wall fresco of Monsieur Paul. Paul would visit Les Halles every day, often parking his jeep out front on the sidewalk. The police knew his car and didn't fine him. He would have coffee with the cheese lady and the meat lady and then often head to the estate of his mistress to hunt (this caused a bit of an uproar when it came out in his biography, even in France). After he would return home to his restaurant L'Auberge du Pont de Collonges, housed in his childhood home. He died there in 2017 at the age of 91.

You could call Paul Bocuse the first celebrity chef. Before him, the cooks were hidden in the kitchen, after Monsieur Paul, the cooks became stars.

About the Author

Paul den Arend grew up in the Netherlands and has been travelling for most of his adult life. He studied art history in Salamanca, Spain, wrote reports for the Dutch Embassy in Santiago de Chile and studied Chinese in China. In between, he has been working as a tour guide. For many years he lived in Rome, Italy and guided groups of all backgrounds through the city. He has been a guide in the Vatican Museums, Saint Peter's and the Galleria Borghese, but he also loves to show groups around Sicily or Tuscany. His guidebooks reflect a profound love for the Eternal City and the many stories about its beautiful piazza's and landmarks.

Printed in Great Britain
by Amazon